WALKS
IN

THREE PEAKS
COUNTRY

HILLSIDE GUIDES

LONG DISTANCE WALKS

1 • THE WESTMORLAND WAY
2 • THE FURNESS WAY
3 • THE CUMBERLAND WAY
7 • CLEVELAND WAY COMPANION
9 • THE NORTH BOWLAND TRAVERSE
   (by David Johnson)
16 • DALES WAY COMPANION

CIRCULAR WALKS - YORKSHIRE DALES

4 • WALKS IN WHARFEDALE
5 • WALKS IN NIDDERDALE
6 • WALKS IN THE CRAVEN DALES
8 • WALKS IN WENSLEYDALE
10 • WALKS IN THREE PEAKS COUNTRY
11 • WALKS IN SWALEDALE
20 • RAMBLES IN WHARFEDALE
21 • WALKS ON THE HOWGILL FELLS

CIRCULAR WALKS - NORTH YORK MOORS

13 • WESTERN - Cleveland/Hambleton Hills
14 • SOUTHERN - Rosedale/Farndale/Bransdale
15 • NORTHERN - Eskdale and the Coast

CIRCULAR WALKS - SOUTH PENNINES

12 • WALKS IN BRONTE COUNTRY
17 • WALKS IN CALDERDALE

HILLWALKING - THE LAKE DISTRICT

18 • OVER LAKELAND MOUNTAINS
19 • OVER LAKELAND FELLS

———

FREEDOM OF THE DALES
40 selected walks
Full colour hardback

WALKS
IN
THREE PEAKS
COUNTRY

by

Paul Hannon

HILLSIDE  PUBLICATIONS

HILLSIDE PUBLICATIONS
11 Nessfield Grove
Exley Head
Keighley
West Yorkshire
BD22 6NU

First published in 1987
as 'Walks in the Western Dales'
Fully revised (3rd impression) with the
addition of new material 1991

Page 1 illustration: on Smearsett Scar

ISBN   1   870141   13 X

Printed in Great Britain by
Carnmor Print and Design
95/97 London Road
Preston
Lancashire
PR1 4BA

INTRODUCTION

Stainforth Bridge

The south-western corner of the Yorkshire Dales is an area dominated by remarkable limestone formations and high mountains, to the extent that the triumvirate of most famous peaks have given their collective title to the district. As in the rest of the Dales, however it is the valleys that really shape the countryside, and the two major dales are those of the Dee and the Ribble. Rising on the same moorland they immediately assume opposite directions, the Dee running north to Sedbergh and the Ribble south to Settle. They share a common disregard for Yorkshire, for these days Dentdale is wholly Cumbrian, and the Ribble is destined to be one of Lancashire's major rivers. A cluster of short valleys drain the country from Settle to Kirkby Lonsdale, where the broad Lune makes a borderline appearance.

Whernside, Ingleborough or Penyghent - often all three - are regular backdrops to most scenes in the district, for they are truly its heart, and walkers come from afar to face their collective challenge, even though they offer far more enjoyable individual walks. As a result it is, ironically, often quieter nearer the valleys. This theory is tested in this collection of rambles, for the Three Peaks themselves are only a part of the mountain scene hereabouts, and rather more demanding ascents of these summits have therefore been left aside to be dealt with in a more appropriate volume.

In these pages, hard going on the peaty heights is largely forsaken for the glories of limestone country. Instead, we have an array of gleaming scars and pavements, an unparalleled assembly of gaping potholes and labyrinthian caves, and a series of inviting green trackways over the hills. Dentdale, meanwhile, as northern limit of our area, remains enviously enshrouded in near-timelessness.

When special trains run, the Settle-Carlisle Railway is also enshrouded - in steam. Running the length of Ribblesdale and encircling the head of Dentdale, this monument to Victorian

THE ROAD NETWORK

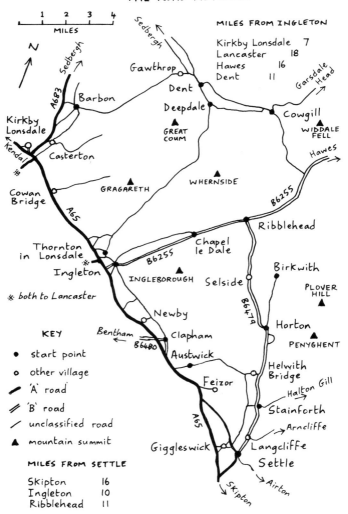

MILES

MILES FROM INGLETON

Kirkby Lonsdale	7
Lancaster	18
Hawes	16
Dent	11

* both to Lancaster

KEY

●	start point
○	other village
▬	'A' road
⫽	'B' road
╱	unclassified road
▲	mountain summit

MILES FROM SETTLE

Skipton	16
Ingleton	10
Ribblehead	11

6

enterprise is as much a part of the district as the very hills. It is hard now to conceive of its demise, yet it was only in 1989 that the finest line in England was saved from shameful closure. It offers the grandest approach to Three Peaks Country, and is aided by the Skipton-Lancaster line in the south of the area.

Also passing through the district are no less than three long-distance footpaths, the long-established Pennine and Dales Ways, now joined by the Ribble Way.

Detailed overleaf is a miscellany of information, though some services — buses in particular — are sparse, or perhaps only seasonal. Further accommodation can be found by way of youth hostels at Dentdale, Ingleton and Stainforth, while there are bunkbarns at Dub Cote, Horton and at Chapel le Dale. Camping sites are liberally scattered throughout the area.

	Market Day	Early Closing
Ingleton	Friday	Thursday
Kirkby Lonsdale	Thursday	Wednesday
Settle	Tuesday	Wednesday

The 16 walks described range in length from 4¼ to 9½ miles, and the terrain similarly varies from riverside strolls to rather more strenuous moorland outings. All walks are circular, and with an average distance of 6½ miles are ideally suited to half-day rambles. Each walk is given its own chapter consisting of 'immediate impression' diagram, detailed narrative and strip-map and notes and illustrations of features of interest along the way.

ORDNANCE SURVEY MAPS

Although the strip-maps illustrating each walk are sufficient to guide one safely around, they cannot depict the surrounding countryside, nor show the adjoining paths should one wish to amend any particular route. An Ordnance Survey map will thus make an ideal companion.

All but one of the walks are covered by only one map at both 1:25,000 and 1:50,000 scales: -
1:50,000 - Landranger sheet 98
1:25,000 - Outdoor Leisure Map 2 (Yorkshire Dales West)
The misfit is Walk 2, covered on:
1:50,000 - Landranger sheet 97
1:25,000 - Pathfinder sheet 628 (SD 67/68)

7

SOME USEFUL FACILITIES

	Rail station	Accommodation	Inn	Car park	Bus service	Post office	other shop	WC	Payphone
Austwick		•	•		•	•			•
Barbon		•	•		•		•		•
Chapel le Dale		•	•		•				•
Clapham	•	•	•	•	•	•	•	•	•
Cowgill/Dent Head	•※	•	•		•				•
Deepdale Foot		•							•
Dent		•	•	•	•	•	•	•	•
Gawthrop		•					•		•
Helwith Bridge		•	•		•				•
Horton	•	•	•	•	•	•	•		•
Ingleton		•	•	•	•	•	•	•	•
Langcliffe		•		•	•	•			•
Ribblehead	•※	•	•		•				
Selside		•							•
Settle	•	•	•		•	•	•	•	•
Stainforth		•	•	•	•	•	•	•	•
Thornton		•	•						•

※ The station near Cowgill is known as Dent, and that at Ribblehead is currently southbound only

A rough guide only

8

SOME USEFUL ADDRESSES

Ramblers' Association
   1/5 Wandsworth Road, London SW8 2XX
      Tel. 071-582 6878

Youth Hostels Association
   Trevelyan House, St. Albans, Herts. AL1 2DY
      Tel. 0727-55215

Yorkshire Dales National Park Office
   Colvend, Hebden Road, Grassington, Skipton BD23 5LB
      Tel. 0756-752748

Clapham National Park Centre - Car Park
      Tel. 05242-51419

Horton Tourist Information - Penyghent Cafe
      Tel. 0729-860333

Ingleton Tourist Information - Community Centre
      Tel. 05242-41049

Settle Tourist Information - Town Hall
      Tel. 0729-825192

Yorkshire Dales Society
   Otley Civic Centre, Cross Green, Otley LS21 1HD
      Tel. 0943-607868

British Rail, Skipton   0756-792543

Yorkshire Dales weather   0898-500 748

Bus services:

   Pennine Motors, Gargrave   0756-749215

   Cumberland Motor Services, Kendal   0539-733221

   Ribble Motor Services, Lancaster   0524-64228

   Keighley + District Travel, Skipton   0756-795331

   Whaites Coaches, Settle   0729-823235

THE WALKS

Listed below are the 16 walks described, the walk number being the key to easy location in the guide

THE WALKS

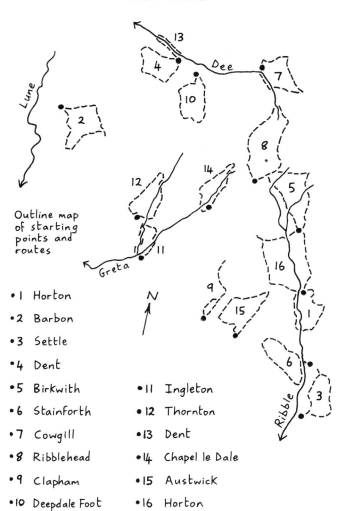

Outline map
of starting
points and
routes

- 1 Horton
- 2 Barbon
- 3 Settle
- 4 Dent
- 5 Birkwith
- 6 Stainforth
- 7 Cowgill
- 8 Ribblehead
- 9 Clapham
- 10 Deepdale Foot
- 11 Ingleton
- 12 Thornton
- 13 Dent
- 14 Chapel le Dale
- 15 Austwick
- 16 Horton

WALK 1

6½ miles

THE HEART OF RIBBLESDALE

from Horton-in-Ribblesdale

An excellent introduction to the various features of the dale in the neighbourhood of Horton

National Park car park in the village centre

THE WALK

Leave the car park by the footbridge at its north end to by-pass the narrow road bridges by the Crown Hotel. Across the Ribble, take a stile on the left to follow the river downstream. The way remains with its bank past Cragg Hill Farm, where a basic footbridge is unlikely to offer any temptation to cross. When the field boundary beyond the farm parts company, branch away from the river to join a sunken lane which is quickly enclosed by walls. After passing beneath the railway, it meets a road which is followed left towards Helwith Bridge. With the inn in sight, take a stile to cross a field to emerge onto the road by way of its car park.

Cross the bridge to a junction, and go left along the main valley road a few yards before branching right up a walled lane. When this rough lane forks, bear left to commence a long, easy march up a splendid green way. Eventually it runs free, but when a crumbling wall appears on the left, it is almost time to opt for a level, equally pleasurable way branching off the main track. It descends quickly to a gate, but it is a stile in the bottom corner of the pasture that is the key to concluding the descent to the lane at Dub Cote Farm.

Turn right along this narrow byway, keeping right

at a junction to pass through Brackenbottom and circuitously round to Horton's school. Though we are now back into the village, there is one further sight before finishing. Cross the footbridge and turn right, then fork left along a track which soon joins a similar walled track. Head right as far as a gate on the left 100 yards past a seat, and cross fields to a prominent clump of trees marking Brants Gill Head.

A stile in the wall right of the trees admits to the vicinity of the beck head, which is seen to better advantage by a scramble down the slope. Above and behind the beck can be found another wall-stile: head directly away to a gate to join another walled track. This is Harber Scar Lane, which drops down into the village to emerge alongside the Crown Hotel.

Horton in Ribblesdale is the highest village in a valley which ends in the Irish Sea beyond Preston, and it is the centre of Three Peaks country. It has no intrinsic charm, being a curious mixture of dwellings strung along the road, and of course overlooked by a horrendous quarry. Horton's real attraction is its location, as the sight of countless boots being pulled on in its overfaced car park will testify: the place has a true walkers' atmosphere.

A renowned cafe caters for the weary, while inns are found at either end. One has two arched bridges outside, while the other faces St. Oswald's church: this displays work as far back as Norman times, while the solid-looking tower has leanings towards Pisa.

Penyghent from Horton

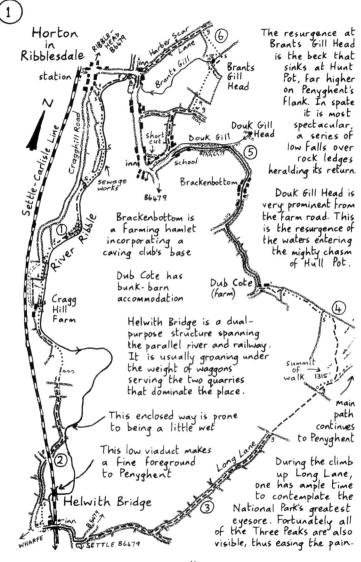

Horton in Ribblesdale

station

RIBBLE-HEAD B6479

Settle-Carlisle Line

N

Cragghill Road

River Ribble

Harber Scar Lane

⑥

inn

Brants Gill

Brants Gill Head

Short cut

Douk Gill Head

Douk Gill

⑤

inn

school

Brackenbottom

B6479

sewage works

Cragg Hill Farm

Dub Cote (farm)

④

summit of walk 1315

main path continues to Penyghent

Long Lane

③

②

Helwith Bridge

inn

B6479

WHARFE

SETTLE B6479

The resurgence at Brants Gill Head is the beck that sinks at Hunt Pot, far higher on Penyghent's flank. In spate it is most spectacular, a series of low falls over rock ledges heralding its return.

Douk Gill Head is very prominent from the farm road. This is the resurgence of the waters entering the mighty chasm of Hull Pot.

Brackenbottom is a farming hamlet incorporating a caving club's base

Dub Cote has bunk-barn accommodation

Helwith Bridge is a dual-purpose structure spanning the parallel river and railway. It is usually groaning under the weight of waggons serving the two quarries that dominate the place.

This enclosed way is prone to being a little wet

This low viaduct makes a fine foreground to Penyghent

During the climb up Long Lane, one has ample time to contemplate the National Park's greatest eyesore. Fortunately all of the Three Peaks are also visible, thus easing the pain.

WALK 2

8½ miles

from Barbon

A stunning combination of
first-rate Dales
scenery – except
it's all 'outside'
the Dales!

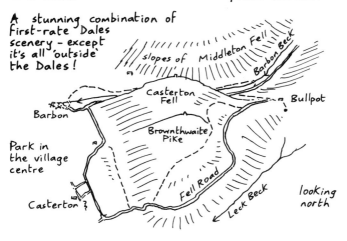

THE WALK

Leave the village by the drive to Barbon Manor, just past the church. It crosses Barbon Beck and begins to climb through Barbon Park, then part-way up a sign indicates a green track heading right into the trees. Lively Barbon Beck is followed all the way through the wood, remaining with it through a large pasture to a sheepfold. Just a little further, a simple footbridge conveys us to the road on the other side.

Turn right a short way until the road runs free, and after crossing Aygill take the second green track sloping back up to the left. This clear track scales the lower contours of Casterton Fell to eventually become enclosed at a saddle, just prior to which Aygill breaks into a ravine that earns a detour. The track runs on to the terminus of the surfaced Fell Road at Bullpot Farm. While the road is our route, a detour to see Bullpot's hole can quickly be made: a wicket-gate at the end of the house is the key to a cavers' path along the wall-side to Bull Pot of the Witches.

Back at the road-end, head along its traffic-free way as far as a bend on a minor brow, with Gale Garth Farm below.

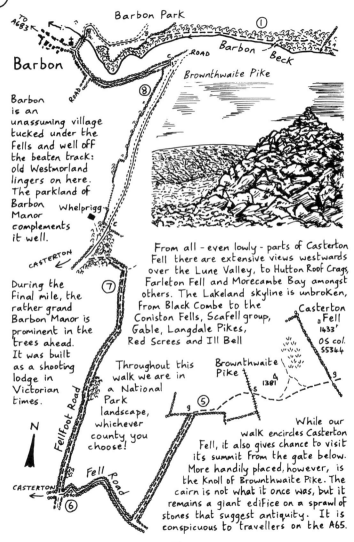

To A683

Barbon Park

① Barbon Beck

ROAD

Brownthwaite Pike

Barbon

ROAD

⑧

Barbon is an unassuming village tucked under the fells and well off the beaten track: old Westmorland lingers on here. The parkland of Barbon Manor complements it well.

Whelprigg

CASTERTON

During the final mile, the rather grand Barbon Manor is prominent in the trees ahead. It was built as a shooting lodge in Victorian times.

⑦

N

CASTERTON

Fellfoot Road

Throughout this walk we are in a National Park landscape, whichever county you choose!

Fell Road

CASTERTON

⑥

From all - even lowly - parts of Casterton Fell there are extensive views westwards over the Lune Valley, to Hutton Roof Crags, Farleton Fell and Morecambe Bay amongst others. The Lakeland skyline is unbroken, from Black Combe to the Coniston Fells, Scafell group, Gable, Langdale Pikes, Red Screes and Ill Bell.

Casterton Fell 1433' OS col. SS344

Brownthwaite Pike
△ 1381
S
g

⑤
g

While our walk encircles Casterton Fell, it also gives chance to visit it's summit from the gate below. More handily placed, however, is the knoll of Brownthwaite Pike. The cairn is not what it once was, but it remains a giant edifice on a sprawl of stones that suggest antiquity. It is conspicuous to travellers on the A65.

16

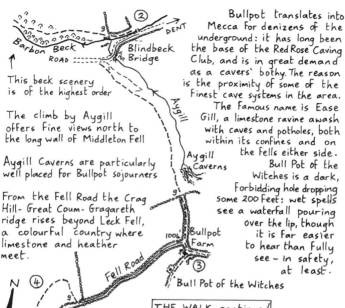

Bullpot translates into Mecca for denizens of the underground: it has long been the base of the Red Rose Caving Club, and is in great demand as a cavers' bothy. The reason is the proximity of some of the finest cave systems in the area.

The famous name is Ease Gill, a limestone ravine awash with caves and potholes, both within its confines and on the fells either side.

Bull Pot of the Witches is a dark, forbidding hole dropping some 200 feet: wet spells see a waterfall pouring over the lip, though it is far easier to hear than fully see – in safety, at least.

This beck scenery is of the highest order

The climb by Aygill offers fine views north to the long wall of Middleton Fell

Aygill Caverns are particularly well placed for Bullpot sojourners

From the Fell Road the Crag Hill- Great Coum- Gragareth ridge rises beyond Leck Fell, a colourful country where limestone and heather meet.

THE WALK continued

Here take the second of two gates on the right, from where a clear track heads away. Curving round the grassy flank of Casterton Fell it rises steadily and splendidly to a gate: set well back up to the right is the Ordnance column marking the summit. Through the gate the monster cairn on Brownthwaite Pike looms ahead, demanding a detour from the track. The green way, meanwhile, runs gradually down to a wall, to leave the fell by way of a smashing green lane that descends in Roman fashion back to the Fell Road.

Turn down as far as a crossroads with rough lanes, and opt for the one on the right. Initially disturbed by the passage of cattle, it rapidly improves into a magnificent green byway, and also lives up to its title of Fellfoot Road. In the end it joins a back road opposite the large house at Whelprigg, to be followed right to soon run free again along the base of the fell. At the junction at the end, turn left to drop back into the village, which is revealed only at the last moment.

WALK 3 | CATRIGG FORCE AND ATTERMIRE SCAR |

6³⁄₄ miles   from Settle

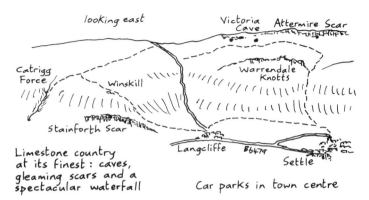

looking east

Victoria Cave   Attermire Scar

Catrigg Force

Winskill

Warrendale Knotts

Stainforth Scar

Langcliffe   B6479

Settle

Limestone country
at its finest: caves,
gleaming scars and a
spectacular waterfall

Car parks in town centre

| THE WALK |

    Leave the market place by Constitution Hill, to the
left of the Shambles. After a steep pull the road turns left,
and almost at once abandon it in favour of the rougher Banks
Lane, to the right. On emerging to cross a field-bottom it is
briefly enclosed again before heading along to a stile on the
left. Head across to find the next stile, then continue along
with another wall before finally dropping left to emerge onto
the road out of Langcliffe.

    Turn into the village, and in order to see something of
the place, take the second lane on the right (opposite the green).
Go straight over an early crossroads to follow an absolute
gem of a green lane all the way to its demise. Opt for the
right-hand gate to run along the field-top, and from the gate
at the far end a way climbs steeply above the lip of an old
quarry. A small gate in the top corner is the key to continuing
up the next smaller enclosure, which is left by a stile right of
a walled track heading left. A field is crossed to empty onto
Lower Winskill's drive, turning right to arrive at the entrance
to High Winskill Farm.

    Our route crosses straight over to the track directly
ahead, which peters out shortly after a stile. Another stile is
soon espied ahead, and from it the detour to Catrigg Force can

be made. Its location is in no doubt, being shrouded in trees at the bottom of the field. A pair of neighbouring stiles lead to the top of the waterfall, where with great care we can peer down to the bottom. The conventional view can be sampled by entering the trees on the left to descend a good path to the foot of the ravine.

On returning to the stile at the top of the large field, bear left along a farm track which rises to join the Malham Moor road. Turn right along this unfenced strip of tarmac as far as a cattle-grid, then strike left along an inviting green track to rise to a stile. After outcrops beyond it turn left up to another stile onto a wide track: up to the left are the entrances to Jubilee Caves.

Follow the track right, but when it heads down the field to the right, maintain a level course on the path along the base of the scar. After a second stile a detour up to the left signals arrival at Victoria Cave, a place to halt. From its enormous entrance another path returns to the main one to resume the journey. After an open pasture the path drops down to a gateway below Attermire Scar, but those intent on locating Attermire Cave should use a thinner path branching left to contour across to arrive just below its modest entrance in the cliff.

Back at the gateway, meanwhile, pass through it and head away from the scar, with the lofty sentinels of Warrendale Knotts up to the right. Beyond a stile and a gateway the way bears right, following the wall past a cave and up to the brow of the hill. Descend to a wall-corner but then continue straight down a steep slope to meet the outward path, going left to quickly re-enter Settle.

Victoria Cave

Jubilee Cave, looking out

Catrigg Force

Settle is a bustling little town which acts as an important focal point for an extensive rural area comprising largely of upper Ribblesdale. It is invariably busy, being a long-established halting place for those bound further afield, and is also ideally centred for the Three Peaks district. Market days present the liveliest scene, when the small square is awash with colour.

The town boasts numerous old buildings, some hidden and others very much on display. Facing the square is the historic row known as the Shambles, with its shops peeping from behind archways. Nearby is The Folly, a large, rambling 17th century house with an intricate facade. Also facing the square is a former inn 'the Naked Man', its appropriate carved sign being dated 1633 and a source of some humour. The Museum of North Craven Life gives a rewarding insight into the district's past while the limestone cliff of Castlebergh provides a dramatic bird's-eye view of the town today. Settle was by-passed by the A65 in 1988.

20

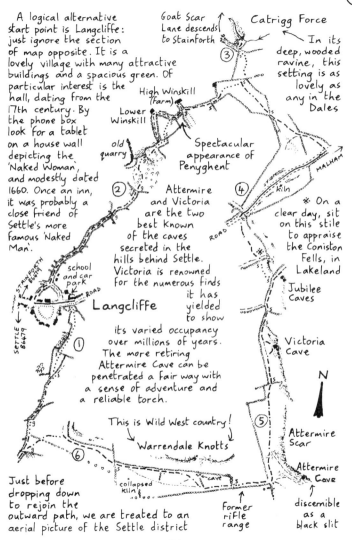

A logical alternative start point is Langcliffe: just ignore the section of map opposite. It is a lovely village with many attractive buildings and a spacious green. Of particular interest is the hall, dating from the 17th century. By the phone box look for a tablet on a house wall depicting the 'Naked Woman', and modestly dated 1660. Once an inn, it was probably a close friend of Settle's more famous 'Naked Man'.

Goat Scar Lane descends to Stainforth

Catrigg Force

In its deep, wooded ravine, this setting is as lovely as any in the Dales

High Winskill (farm)

Lower Winskill

old quarry

Spectacular appearance of Penyghent

MALHAM

kiln

※ On a clear day, sit on this stile to appraise the Coniston Fells, in Lakeland

ROAD

Jubilee Caves

Victoria Cave

N

Attermire Scar

Attermire Cave

discernible as a black slit

Attermire and Victoria are the two best known of the caves secreted in the hills behind Settle. Victoria is renowned for the numerous finds it has yielded to show its varied occupancy over millions of years. The more retiring Attermire Cave can be penetrated a fair way with a sense of adventure and a reliable torch.

school and car park

ROAD

STAINFORTH B6479

SETTLE B6479

Langcliffe

This is Wild West country!

Warrendale Knotts

collapsed kiln

CAVE

Former rifle range

Just before dropping down to rejoin the outward path, we are treated to an aerial picture of the Settle district

21

WALK 4

5'2 miles

from Dent

Beckside and fellside walking combine to give delightful close-hand and majestic distant views

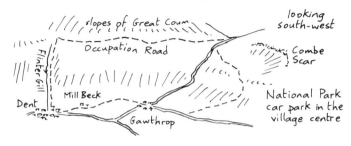

slopes of Great Coum

looking south-west

Occupation Road

Flinter Gill

Combe Scar

Dent

Mill Beck

National Park car park in the village centre

Gawthrop

THE WALK

From the car park cross the road and take the one rising past the memorial hall. At a delightful grouping of cottages at the foot of Flinter Gill it becomes a stony track to start climbing above the beck. On opening out it becomes enclosed by walls but pleasanter underfoot to rise up to the Occupation Road. Turn right along this wide, green lane, which becomes gradually stonier before eventually meeting the Dent-Barbon road.

Accompany this briefly right before a footpath sign points the way through a gate on the left. A sketchy track crosses to a stile in the far corner. From it head left towards the steep slope, and a path materialises to swing right as a superb green promenade. All too soon a gateway is reached and the path fades at the sad ruin of Combe House. Pass round the far side and follow a barely discernible wall-line heading away.

Down the field a farm track is joined to head left down through a gateway. Through the next gateway forsake the track and make a bee-line for the farm buildings of Tofts. A slab footbridge over a tree-lined beck precedes a clamber up the opposite bank. Pass between the buildings and out along the drive, dropping gradually down to a back road at Underwood. Gawthrop is just minutes along to the right.

Gawthrop is vacated by the third branch on the right after the bridge (at a phone box). The lane swings to the left between houses: after crossing another beck fork right, but within yards take an enclosed path left in front of a short row of cottages to rejoin the wider track by a barn. Take the gate to its right and head directly away through several fields to descend to a track to the Farm complex at Mill Beck.

Remain on the track through the buildings, it becoming the drive to head away down to the road. Part-way, however, it passes a lone house, and here take two gates on the right to cross the bottoms of several fields to a large modern barn. Squeezing to its left, a field alloted to caravans is entered at High Laning Farm. Head right towards the yard, and then out along its drive to emerge onto the road in Dent adjacent to the Methodist chapel.

Dent Town

On passing through the gateway before the ruinous Combe House, the striking hollow of Combe Scar looms tantalisingly above. This colourful scene — unjustly bereft of a right of way — is chiselled out of the northern flank of Middleton Fell. It is a popular Dentdale landmark, and with its low crags there is more than a hint of Lakeland about it.

Gawthrop is a picturesque grouping of cottages and farms, well off the beaten track

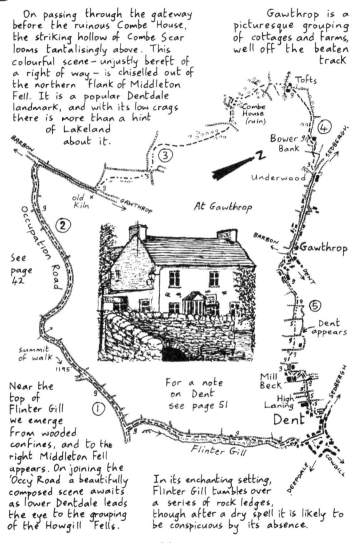

At Gawthrop

See page 42

summit of walk 1195'

Near the top of Flinter Gill we emerge from wooded confines, and to the right Middleton Fell appears. On joining the 'Occy Road a beautifully composed scene awaits as lower Dentdale leads the eye to the grouping of the Howgill Fells.

For a note on Dent see page 51

In its enchanting setting, Flinter Gill tumbles over a series of rock ledges, though after a dry spell it is likely to be conspicuous by its absence.

24

WALK 5

7 miles

LING GILL AND THORNS GILL

from Birkwith

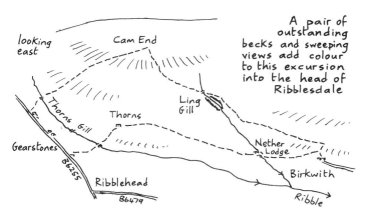

looking east

Cam End

Thorns Gill

Thorns

Ling Gill

Gearstones

B6255

Nether Lodge

Ribblehead

B6479

Birkwith

Ribble

A pair of outstanding becks and sweeping views add colour to this excursion into the head of Ribblesdale

At High Birkwith Farm (terminus of the surfaced road from the bridge by the Crown at Horton) ask permission to park, paying a small fee and then driving up the rough road towards Old Ing.

THE WALK

The rough road from High Birkwith climbs past Old Ing to a gate to meet the Pennine Way. This is followed left all the way to Cam End: the track is clear throughout, if a little rough and stony, and in parts wet. An enclosed spell leads at once to Calf Holes, while next feature of much interest is Ling Gill. Beyond its head the beck is crossed at Ling Gill Bridge, and the way then meanders about before rising to Cam End. A guidepost set into a cairn marks this major junction, and our way is left, now astride the Dales Way.

At the foot of the fell Gayle Beck is crossed by a high and long footbridge, then crossing to a stile and up to the road at Far Gearstones. Go left past Gearstones and on until a barn grouping in the field below signals the moment to take a hand-gate (signposted to Nether Lodge). Follow the left-hand wall down to cross Thorns Gill by way of a delicate packhorse bridge. Ignoring the out-of-date graffiti on the boulders, rise half-left, and on the brow head away to the barns amid a cluster of trees at Thorns.

A short enclosed way leads to a junction in front of the main barn, and here take a slim gate on the right into a small enclosure. From the stile opposite head up by the wall-side to the brow of Back Hools Hill, to then drop down to a barn. From the gate there a soggy track slants across to the next stile: on moorland again, a thin path heads away, dropping to a beck and rising to a fence from where Nether Lodge appears ahead. Opt for the less obvious left-hand path making a bee-line for the farm.

Take the enclosed way to the right of the house, bear left to cross the bridge and left again to a stile. A stony track rises away to lose itself on a brow, before we drop to a stile at God's Bridge. A path heads away to be joined by a track, which beyond a final stile either runs on to the farm road above High Birkwith, or is vacated for the steep grassy slope to finish just below Old Ing.

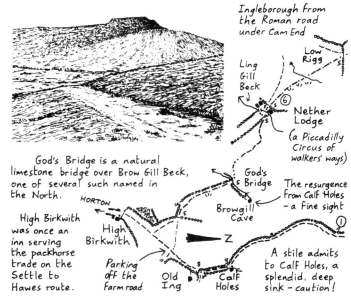

Ingleborough from the Roman road under Cam End

Low Rigg

Ling Gill Beck

⑥ Nether Lodge

(a Piccadilly Circus of walkers' ways)

God's Bridge is a natural limestone bridge over Brow Gill Beck, one of several such named in the North.

HORTON

God's Bridge

The resurgence from Calf Holes – a fine sight

Browgill Cave

High Birkwith was once an inn serving the packhorse trade on the Settle to Hawes route.

High Birkwith

Parking off the farm road

Old Ing

Z

Calf Holes

A stile admits to Calf Holes, a splendid, deep sink - caution!

①

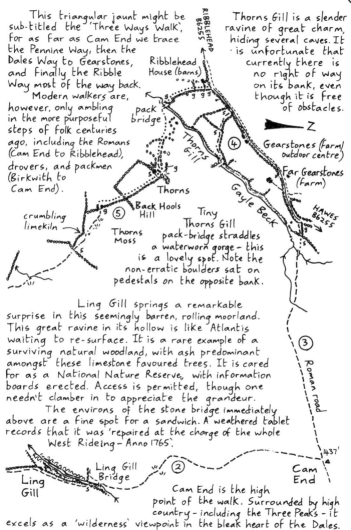

This triangular jaunt might be sub-titled the 'Three Ways Walk', for as far as Cam End we trace the Pennine Way, then the Dales Way to Gearstones, and finally the Ribble Way most of the way back.

Modern walkers are, however, only ambling in the more purposeful steps of folk centuries ago, including the Romans (Cam End to Ribblehead), drovers, and packmen (Birkwith to Cam End).

Thorns Gill is a slender ravine of great charm, hiding several caves. It is unfortunate that currently there is no right of way on its bank, even though it is free of obstacles.

RIBBLEHEAD B6255

Ribblehead House (barns)

pack bridge

Thorns Gill

Thorns

Back Hools Hill

crumbling limekiln

Thorns Moss

④

⑤

Gearstones (farm/ outdoor centre)

Far Gearstones (farm)

Gayle Beck

HAWES B6255

Tiny Thorns Gill pack-bridge straddles a waterworn gorge - this is a lovely spot. Note the non-erratic boulders sat on pedestals on the opposite bank.

Ling Gill springs a remarkable surprise in this seemingly barren, rolling moorland. This great ravine in its hollow is like Atlantis waiting to re-surface. It is a rare example of a surviving natural woodland, with ash predominant amongst these limestone favoured trees. It is cared for as a National Nature Reserve, with information boards erected. Access is permitted, though one needn't clamber in to appreciate the grandeur.

The environs of the stone bridge immediately above are a fine spot for a sandwich. A weathered tablet records that it was 'repaired at the charge of the whole West Riding - Anno 1765'.

Ling Gill

Ling Gill Bridge

②

③

Roman road

1437'

Cam End

Cam End is the high point of the walk. Surrounded by high country - including the Three Peaks - it excels as a 'wilderness' viewpoint in the bleak heart of the Dales.

WALK 6 — SMEARSETT, FEIZOR AND THE RIBBLE

7½ miles — from Stainforth

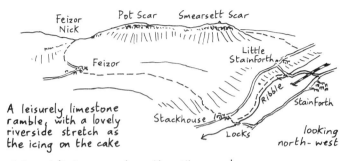

Feizor Nick — Pot Scar — Smearsett Scar — Little Stainforth — Ribble — Stainforth — Stackhouse — Locks

A leisurely limestone ramble, with a lovely riverside stretch as the icing on the cake

looking north-west

National Park car park in the village centre

THE WALK

From the car park turn right along the main road, leaving it almost immediately by a narrow road to the left. Bridging the railway, it descends to cross Stainforth Bridge and then up to a junction at Little Stainforth. Turn right as far as a bend where a track rises to a barn on the left. At a wall-corner up behind the barn a stile is located, and the way rises up through stiles in three intervening walls. From the last one no more are visible: here continue straight over the gentle brow, with the slope on the left rising up to the Ordnance column atop Smearsett Scar.

The grassy slope gives no hint of the grandeur of its other side, but as there is no public right of way to its top, the route simply crosses the pasture to find the next, more distant stile. Swinging right to the next stile, the path then follows a wall to meet the rough lane through Feizor Nick. Go left to drop down into Feizor itself.

Follow the road only part-way through, then take a rough track on the left between barns. Beyond a gate a broad track rises ever gradually away, and rather sketchily when the wall parts company. Eventually a stile is reached, and the way keeps on through two gates. Just after the second, take a gate on the right to resume the journey. Beyond the next gate the track zigzags down through a gateway where it fades completely. Head straight down the field where a choice of stiles precede a steeper drop to the edge of Stackhouse. Go right with its boundary wall, and a mucky path runs through the trees to a stile onto a back road.

Turn left past the two entrances to Stackhouse, and then take a green lane to the right to meet the Ribble at the Locks. Don't use the footbridge (other than as a view -point), but turn upstream with the river. At the end of a long pasture after Langcliffe paper mill we are briefly parted from the Ribble, but that aside, its bank leads unerringly back to Stainforth Bridge. Just before it, however, the waterplay of Stainforth Force will undoubtedly delay the walk's conclusion. It ends as it began, up the road and back into the village.

Little Stainforth, also known as Knight Stainforth, is today just a tiny hamlet, and a kid brother to the main village across the river. Noteworthy is the austere hall dating largely from the 17th century, and on the site of an older building.

Knight Stainforth Hall

Feizor is an unspoilt settlement at the terminus for motor vehicles of a short cul-de-sac to this hollow in the hills. Footpaths, however, radiate in all directions. Note the lovely corner with a water pump and trough sat on a tiny green outside a row of cottages.

From here, Ingleborough is ranged magnificently beyond Norber and Crummackdale

A splendid traditional limestone-based woodland

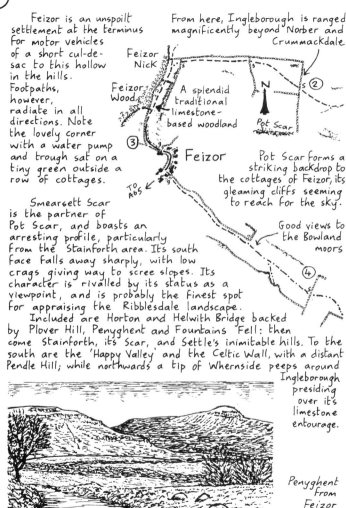

Pot Scar forms a striking backdrop to the cottages of Feizor, its gleaming cliffs seeming to reach for the sky.

Smearsett Scar is the partner of Pot Scar, and boasts an arresting profile, particularly from the Stainforth area. Its south face falls away sharply, with low crags giving way to scree slopes. Its character is rivalled by its status as a viewpoint, and is probably the finest spot for appraising the Ribblesdale landscape.

Good views to the Bowland moors

Included are Horton and Helwith Bridge backed by Plover Hill, Penyghent and Fountains Fell: then come Stainforth, its Scar, and Settle's inimitable hills. To the south are the 'Happy Valley' and the Celtic Wall, with a distant Pendle Hill; while northwards a tip of Whernside peeps around Ingleborough presiding over its limestone entourage.

Penyghent from Feizor Nick

Stainforth is a sizeable village stood high above and back from the Ribble, and long since by-passed by the road up the dale. Centrally located are a pleasant multi-roomed inn sporting a popular local name, and the 19th century church of St. Peter. A particularly pleasing corner can be found where stepping stones cross the beck by a small green.

Stainforth's better known features, however, are located outside the village, including an 18th century mansion currently serving as a youth hostel.

HELWITH BRIDGE

1191' Smearsett Scar

①

HORTON &6149 CARLISLE

Stainforth

ARNCLIFFE

SETTLE

car park

SETTLE &6149

At Stainforth Force the combination of bridge, riverbank, waterfall and adjacent caravan site make this a place of popular resort. The falls are indeed idyllically sited, and are a rare burst of activity for the Ribble.

The graceful 17th century bridge was built to serve the York to Lancaster packhorse trade.

Little Stainforth

Hall

caravan site

STACKHOUSE

⑦ Stainforth Force

Witness here the confluence of inflowing Stainforth Beck

An easy error is to continue with the wall to these outcrops, which offer an excellent view to Penyghent

River Ribble

paper mill

⑤

Stackhouse

⑥

Stackhouse is a cosy little grouping of rather exclusive dwellings, huddling beneath the hill and clearly happy to remain hidden in its protective surround of greenery

ROAD

N

weir

SETTLE

Locks ← an attractive scene

31

WALK 7

6 miles

ARTENGILL AND GALLOWAY GATE

from Cowgill

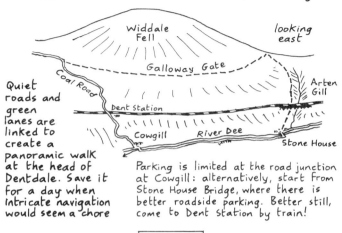

Quiet roads and green lanes are linked to create a panoramic walk at the head of Dentdale. Save it for a day when intricate navigation would seem a chore

Parking is limited at the road junction at Cowgill: alternatively, start from Stone House Bridge, where there is better roadside parking. Better still, come to Dent Station by train!

THE WALK

From Lea Yeat Bridge, Cowgill, head up the steep road to Dent Station. The gradient eases and the Coal Road remains underfoot until virtually level, when branch off right along the enclosed green way of Galloway Gate. This magnificent track contours the western flank of Widdale Fell to eventually drop a short way onto the Arten Gill bridleway. Turn right down this rougher, mostly enclosed track to meet the road at Stone House. Cross the bridge to accompany it and the river Dee back to Cowgill.

The Sportsmans, Cow Dub

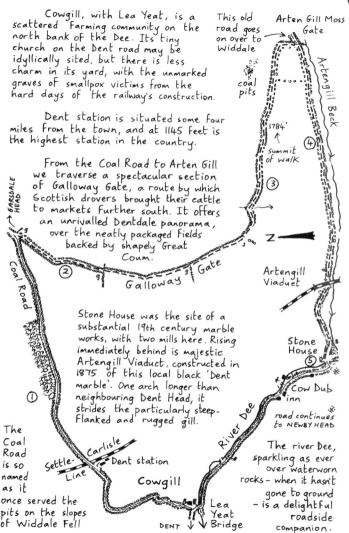

Cowgill, with Lea Yeat, is a scattered farming community on the north bank of the Dee. Its tiny church on the Dent road may be idyllically sited, but there is less charm in its yard, with the unmarked graves of smallpox victims from the hard days of the railway's construction.

Dent station is situated some four miles from the town, and at 1145 feet is the highest station in the country.

From the Coal Road to Arten Gill we traverse a spectacular section of Galloway Gate, a route by which Scottish drovers brought their cattle to markets further south. It offers an unrivalled Dentdale panorama, over the neatly packaged fields backed by shapely Great Coum.

This old road goes on over to Widdale

Arten Gill Moss Gate

Artengill Beck

coal pits

1784'

summit of walk

④

③

FARSDALE HEAD

Coal Road

②

Galloway Gate

Artengill Viaduct

Stone House was the site of a substantial 19th century marble works, with two mills here. Rising immediately behind is majestic Artengill Viaduct, constructed in 1875 of this local black 'Dent marble'. One arch longer than neighbouring Dent Head, it strides the particularly steep-flanked and rugged gill.

Stone House

⑤

Cow Dub inn

road continues to NEWBY HEAD

①

The Coal Road is so named as it once served the pits on the slopes of Widdale Fell

Settle-Carlisle Line

Dent station

Cowgill

Lea Yeat Bridge

DENT ↓ ↓

River Dee

The river Dee, sparkling as ever over waterworn rocks - when it hasn't gone to ground - is a delightful roadside companion.

33

WALK 8

9 miles

BLEA MOOR AND DENT HEAD

from Ribblehead

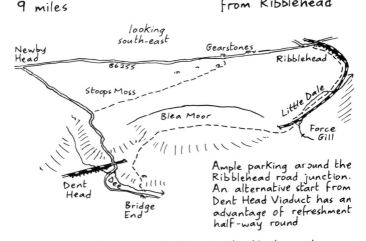

looking south-east

Newby Head

B6255

Gearstones

Ribblehead

Stoops Moss

Little Dale

Blea Moor

Force Gill

Dent Head

Dee

Bridge End

Ample parking around the Ribblehead road junction. An alternative start from Dent Head Viaduct has an advantage of refreshment half-way round

An invigorating march through the bleak country at the heads of two valleys. Not for the genteel!

THE WALK

From the road junction a path runs along to meet the broad track heading for the viaduct. Just before its arches branch right on a clear path which runs parallel to the railway line. This situation continues for a long spell, passing Blea Moor signal box and straying a little from the railway before crossing it by the last bridge (an aqueduct, in fact) before Blea Moor Tunnel. Within yards a fork is reached, each path branching to a different stile in the same fence. While our stile is the right-hand one, the left-hand (main) path yields the splendid view of Force Gill.

Back at the stile above the railway tunnel, a pathless course is set for the spoil heap across the trickle of Little Dale Beck. A good path is joined to trace the tunnel's route past more spoil and attendant air shafts to the top of the moor. Levelling out, a stile in a boundary fence is reached, and the path now descends past another air shaft, through a plantation down to the northern entrance to the tunnel.

From a stile drop down to the line, the path soon moving away from it through a gateway to a footbridge. Just a little downstream the farmyard of disappointingly empty Dent Head is entered, and left by the bridge to the right of the house. Bear half-right across the large field behind to find a stile in the far bottom corner, below which an attractive farm bridge leads onto the road at Bridge End.

This is the most distant point of the walk, and to begin the return head up the steep, winding road, passing Dent Head Viaduct and eventually levelling out beyond a milestone. A little further on a stile on the right sees an undulating path head off past Stoops Moss. Two fences are met in rapid succession and the way soon improves into a pleasanter green track.

On approaching a wall-corner branch right off the main track to remain on the edge of the moor above High Gayle Farm. When the wall drops away follow it down to the dwellings at Winshaw, then out along the drive to meet the Ingleton-Hawes road at Far Gearstones.

Turn right along it for a long mile's march back to Ribblehead, passing the settlement of Gearstones on the way. This is not the tortuous conclusion that might be expected, for much of the tarmac can be spurned in favour of the grass verges.

Ribblehead stands at the junction of two important Dales roads, where that from Ribblesdale meets the arrow-like Ingleton-Hawes road, of Roman origin. The only buildings here are the inn and some cottages by the railway.

It is of course the railway that has earned national fame for Ribblehead, in the shape of its 24-arch viaduct. This noble symbol of Victorian enthusiasm and engineering skills also became the symbol of an outstanding campaign to prevent the closure of the line, and it brings a warm glow to see the scaffolding being used for repairs, and not merely to prop it up!

Force Gill boasts two fine waterfalls, and it is the lower of these that is excellently portrayed from the path to the upper stile. This short section of path has been crudely paved, one of several methods applied to protect the paths from the excesses of erosion caused by 'Three Peakers'.

The main track here is a former packhorse route, the Craven Way. It continues over the hill into Dentdale.

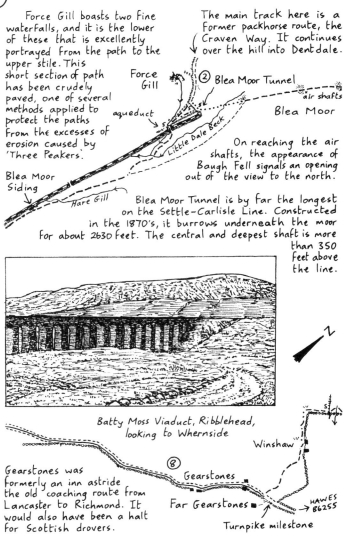

Force Gill

aqueduct

Little Dale Beck

② Blea Moor Tunnel

air shafts

Blea Moor

Blea Moor Siding

Hare Gill

On reaching the air shafts, the appearance of Baugh Fell signals an opening out of the view to the north.

Blea Moor Tunnel is by far the longest on the Settle-Carlisle Line. Constructed in the 1870's, it burrows underneath the moor for about 2630 feet. The central and deepest shaft is more than 350 feet above the line.

Batty Moss Viaduct, Ribblehead, looking to Whernside

Winshaw

⑧ Gearstones

Far Gearstones

Turnpike milestone

HAWES B6255

Gearstones was formerly an inn astride the old coaching route from Lancaster to Richmond. It would also have been a halt for Scottish drovers.

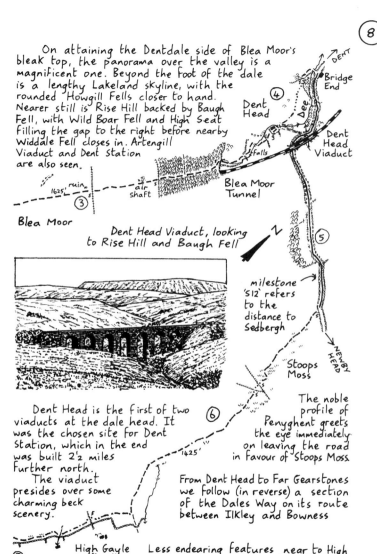

On attaining the Dentdale side of Blea Moor's bleak top, the panorama over the valley is a magnificent one. Beyond the foot of the dale is a lengthy Lakeland skyline, with the rounded Howgill Fells closer to hand. Nearer still is Rise Hill backed by Baugh Fell, with Wild Boar Fell and High Seat filling the gap to the right before nearby Widdale Fell closes in. Artengill Viaduct and Dent Station are also seen.

DENT

Bridge End

(4)

Dent Head

Dee

Dent Head Viaduct

falls

1625' ruin

air shaft

(3)

Blea Moor

Blea Moor Tunnel

Dent Head Viaduct, looking to Rise Hill and Baugh Fell

(5)

milestone '512' refers to the distance to Sedbergh

NEWBY HEAD

Stoops Moss

Dent Head is the first of two viaducts at the dale head. It was the chosen site for Dent Station, which in the end was built 2½ miles further north.
The viaduct presides over some charming beck scenery.

(6)

The noble profile of Penyghent greets the eye immediately on leaving the road in favour of Stoops Moss.

1425'

From Dent Head to Far Gearstones we follow (in reverse) a section of the Dales Way on its route between Ilkley and Bowness

(7)

High Gayle (farm)

Less endearing features near to High Gayle are grouse butts and a rubbish tip

37

WALK 9

| GAPING GILL AND CLAPDALE |

5¾ miles

from Clapham

A straightforward
exploration of the countless
interesting limestone features
hidden in the fine valley
above Clapham

slopes of Ingleborough

Gaping Gill

looking
north-west

Trow
Gill

Clapdale
Farm

Ingleborough Cave

Clapdale

National Park car park in
the village centre

Clapham

| THE WALK |

From the car park cross the footbridge and take
the road up to the right. As it turns left, a gate on the
right leads to the cottage where modest dues must be paid
for entering the private grounds beyond. A wide track goes
right of the cottage and zigzags up to the foot of the lake.
This broad carriageway is now followed the full length of the
valley: after Ingleborough Cave a corner is rounded to climb
through Trow Gill onto the open moor. The path accompanies a
wall, crossing it at the second stile. Just behind it is Bar Pot,
and a few minutes further the path leads a little roughly
and damply to the unmistakable hollow of Gaping Gill.

Having had a good - but cautious - potter around,
retrace steps through Trow Gill to Ingleborough Cave. A little
further on, the return can be varied by taking a path up
to the right just before re-entering the woods. After a
short climb Clapdale Farm is reached: take the stile on the
left to enter its yard, then head directly away along its
access track.

Good views across Clapdale to the broad plateau
of Norber are enjoyed before the track descends (with
views ahead of the Bowland moors) to the edge of Clapham
again, emerging by the ticket cottage. The variation can
be concluded by crossing the first bridge to approach the
church, then turning right for the car park.

Gaping Gill is the great hole, the one that everyone has heard of and that a good number of non-cavers have descended. On the open moor in the lap of Ingleborough, this mighty chasm cannot fail to impress. The innoccuous stream of Fell Beck suddenly falls an unbroken 340 feet from the unfenced lip to the floor of the chamber, which is said to be of sufficient size to hold York Minster. This is no place for skylarking or unrestrained children.

At the two main bank holiday weekends one of two local caving clubs set up a chair and winch to lower the likes of you and me down. If not charged for the descent, you'll have to pay to return to the surface! Several miles of passages radiate from the main chamber, and the course of Fell Beck finally returns to daylight as Clapham Beck, at Beck Head alongside Ingleborough Cave. A connection by cavers was only established in the 1980's after many years efforts.

For the experienced and well-prepared Gaping Gill can be used as a springboard for the ascent of mighty Ingleborough, which looks most inviting in the right conditions.

The wonders of Clapdale include Trow Gill, a former cave and now an overhanging ravine, Gordale in style if not in proportions: unlike Gordale, its valley is dry. Ingleborough Cave is a show cave with guided tours, at least requiring a worthwhile walk to reach it.

In the charming estate grounds is the Grotto, a useful shelter in rain, but the water that will be appreciated is that of the Lake, an artificial tarn locked in glorious woodland.

Clapham is a beautiful village in a setting to match. Thankfully by-passed some years ago, it stands at the foot of Ingleborough from where the waters of Clapham Beck flow to form the centrepiece of the village. Several attractive bridges cross the tree-lined watercourse, and a splendid array of stone cottages line the parallel lane. On the east side of the beck are ranged all the individual features including the inn, the car park and National Park Centre - the old manor house -, the Cave Rescue Organisation HQ, and the church. Dedicated to St. James, its 15th century tower is the best feature.

Near the church is Ingleborough Hall, currently an outdoor centre, but formerly the home of the Farrer family. Best known of them was Reginald (1880 - 1920) who found fame as a botanist, collecting alpine plants on his journeys to far-flung parts and bringing many back to the grounds of the hall. The heavily-wooded grounds and the lake were created by the family earlier in the 19th century. The estate is still privately-owned, hence the small admission fee for enjoying the grounds.

Trow Gill

Gaping Gill

WALK 10

6½ miles

A CIRCUIT OF DEEPDALE

from Deepdale Foot

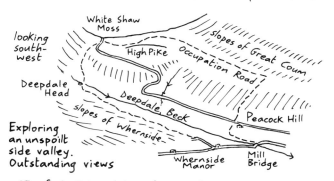

looking south-west

White Shaw Moss

High Pike

slopes of Great Coum

Occupation Road

Deepdale Head

Deepdale Beck

slopes of Whernside

Peacock Hill

Exploring an unspoilt side valley. Outstanding views

Whernside Manor

Mill Bridge

The foot of Deepdale is 1½ miles from Dent. Limited space to park at Mill Bridge, or Whernside Manor just past the Methodist chapel. Alternatively, follow river/beck from Dent

---

THE WALK

Take the narrow lane branching off the road at the Methodist chapel, and remain on its delightful course until it loses its surface at a group of barns. Continuing as a green lane, leave almost at once by a gateway ahead as it swings up to the left. Maintain the level course by crossing the field-top to a part-hidden stile. Generally pathless, the way is marked by a series of charming stiles above Deepdale Beck, and in time a wall comes in on the left to guide us along to Mire Garth Farm.

The route continues along the wall-side, crossing an open pasture after a stile to arrive at Deepdale Head. Don't use the obvious gate but a smaller one just up to the left, to cross a corner of the farmyard to another gate. A steep pull up to the right by stream and then fence leads to a stile onto rougher terrain. A groove runs up to a guidepost, then head half-right up a sketchy path. A small gully is the key to a stile to its left at the top, to emerge on the Ingleton-Dent road just short of its crest.

Turn up the road to the brow and then head off on a broad, walled track to the right. This is the Occupation

Whernside Manor was built about 200 years ago, when it was known as West House. For many years now it has operated as an outdoor recreation centre.

COWGILL

Whernside Manor

Methodist chapel

Mill Bridge

Deepdale Beck

DENT

Deepdale Methodist chapel stands in a typically isolated location, tucked hard by a lane junction embowered in trees.

⑥

Peacock Hill (farm)

DENT ←

Farm

INGLETON

Nun House Outrake

Nun House Outrake gives cause to linger in recognition of its virtues as a Dentdale viewpoint. At the dalehead the railway is seen traversing the flank of Widdale Fell to Dent station, while the valley then leads the eye down to the rounded tops of the Howgill Fells. Only near its foot does the Outrake deteriorate from its green carpet.

The Occupation Road is a walled track which runs across the northern flank of Great Coum, linking the Dent-Ingleton road with that from Gawthrop to Barbon. An old packhorse way, it provides marvellous views from its strictly defined contour.

N

⑤

Occupation Road

THE WALK continued

Road, and apart from a brief spell without walls, it is foolproof as it winds a level course around the hillside. When another walled way eventually appears, follow this– Nun House Outrake– all the way down to the Ingleton-Dent road.

Cross straight over and down a short track by Peacock Hill Farm, crossing over a wider track and a small field behind. From a gate at the far side descend by a hedge to a gate above some barns. Drop left to a stile by the nearest of these to commence a level walk along to the left. At the far end of the pasture is a stile near Deepdale Beck: head on past a small limekiln, rising a little to the next field above a line of trees.

From the next stile head on below a short length of wall, then bear right to the trees masking the beck. A path descends to it to reach Mill Bridge only a matter of yards further downstream. The chapel is just two minutes up the hill over the bridge.

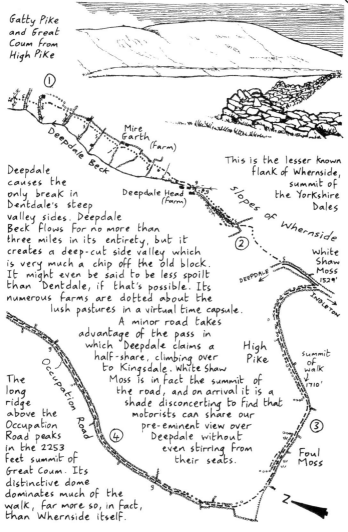

Gatty Pike and Great Coum from High Pike

Mire Garth (farm)

Deepdale Beck

Deepdale Head (farm)

This is the lesser known flank of Whernside, summit of the Yorkshire Dales

slopes of Whernside

DEEPDALE

INGLETON

White Shaw Moss 1529'

High Pike

summit of walk 1710'

Foul Moss

Deepdale causes the only break in Dentdale's steep valley sides. Deepdale Beck flows for no more than three miles in its entirety, but it creates a deep-cut side valley which is very much a chip off the old block. It might even be said to be less spoilt than Dentdale, if that's possible. Its numerous farms are dotted about the lush pastures in a virtual time capsule.

A minor road takes advantage of the pass in which Deepdale claims a half-share, climbing over to Kingsdale. White Shaw Moss is in fact the summit of the road, and on arrival it is a shade disconcerting to find that motorists can share our pre-eminent view over Deepdale without even stirring from their seats.

Occupation Road

The long ridge above the Occupation Road peaks in the 2253 feet summit of Great Coum. Its distinctive dome dominates much of the walk, far more so, in fact, than Whernside itself.

WALK 11

4'4 miles

THE INGLETON GLENS

From Ingleton

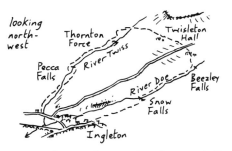

looking north-west

Thornton Force
River Twiss
Pecca Falls
River Doe
Twisleton Hall
Beezley Falls
Snow Falls
Ingleton

A classic, and rightly so. Don't come following a prolonged drought

Descend the steep road by the church, and the entrance and car park are found after the second bridge

Note for the Financially embarrassed: this walk is over private land, and requires a payment at the start

THE WALK

Few directions are needed as the paths are very clear throughout, and the way obvious. From the car park the path heads up the valley of the Twiss, twice crossing the river to arrive at Pecca Falls. A little further is Thornton Force, the walk's highlight, after which another bridge takes the path up to Twisleton Lane. Turn right along its green course to Twisleton Hall, and keeping left of the buildings, using two stiles and a track which descends to a quiet road.

Cross straight over to Beezleys Farm, passing between the buildings to a gate on the left. Drop down to Beezley Falls and follow the river Doe back. Only one crossing on the return, before emerging from the trees high above the river at Cat Leap Fall. The path runs on to a road-end to re-enter the village.

Commonly known as the 'Waterfalls walk', this is one of two famous excursions from Ingleton, the other being an ascent of its hill, Ingleborough. The falls walk has attracted visitors for over a century, and more so than any other in this book, it is worth savouring in one of the winter months when free of the jostling crowds. The paths are everywhere well maintained – justifying the charge – but care is still needed when wet leaves carpet the ground. Be also aware that for a low-level walk, there is a fair amount of 'up and down' work.

The two valleys explored on this walk are remarkably alike, each beautifully wooded and exposing interesting geological features, with the Craven Faults much in evidence. Even without its chief attractions, this would still be a fine walk. For some reason the names of the watercourses have caused confusion. The Twiss is known by some as the Greta, while more curiously Wainwright has transposed the Greta (Twiss) and the Doe. Maybe there's hope for the author yet! What is less in doubt is that at their meeting, if not any earlier, the Greta is born.

Above Thornton Force lies the flat valley floor of Kingsdale, at one time a glacial lake held back by Raven Ray, a good example of a moraine.

Ingleton is famed as the centre for Yorkshire's limestone country, and is certainly a good base for exploring the fells, scars, caves and valleys of the area. The roadside signs proclaiming 'Beauty Spot of the North' may raise the odd smile, but usually only from travellers on the busy A65 which avoids the village centre and its nearby attractions.

The centre of Ingleton is dominated by a long-abandoned railway viaduct. Also prominent is the parish church, and there are numerous interesting little corners to the village. The youth hostel is centrally situated, as are several useful hostelries and shops.

Twisleton Lane offers a grand view to Ingleborough

The 'beauty' of Ingleton, however, must be its location.

Thornton Force

WALK 12 KINGSDALE AND THE TURBARY ROAD

5½ miles

from Thornton in Lonsdale

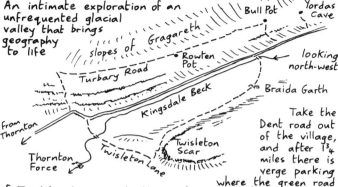

An intimate exploration of an unfrequented glacial valley that brings geography to life

looking north-west

Take the Dent road out of the village, and after 1¾ miles there is verge parking where the green road of Twisleton Lane meets the road. There is further parking a little earlier, before the road descends to this point.

THE WALK

From the junction with Twisleton Lane, head a few yards back in the Thornton direction to a stile on the right. A sketchy path climbs to a ladder-stile on the skyline, clambering through limestone outcrops to reach it, and continuing through more to rise to a complex of ruinous sheepfolds. Up the small gully behind, the outcrops recede, and here incline half-right to meet up with a wall. It rises steadily to meet the Turbary Road at a wall-junction. Turn through the gateway and head off in style along this superb old track, its harder surface soon giving way to a soft grassy base.

The only thing to concentrate on now is ensuring most of the caves in the vicinity of the track are seen, as indicated on the next two pages. Eventually the track foregoes its level course to swing uphill, and here keep straight on along a thin trod to quickly arrive at Bull Pot. Now double back downhill a short way to locate a weakness in the hidden Shout Scar before descending to a gate onto the road.

Turn right along the road until a stile on the left gives access to a footbridge over the dry, stony bed of Kingsdale Beck. Heading for the farm of Braida Garth, cross to a dip behind a prominent knoll, then right through a stile to pass a modern barn before joining the farm's drive. Enter and leave the enclosure in front of the house by way of stiles, then head away through several pathless fields.

From a stile below the end of a wood, a vague path slants up to a stile at a wall-junction, then runs along a wall-side. As a fence takes over, slant slightly left again below a scar to run along to the next stile. Continue to rise through the saddle ahead, on to a collapsed wall and a stile just behind. Just beyond, a superior green track is joined to descend to Twisleton Lane, which is followed right to return to the start.

'Turbary' is the right of commoners to dig peat for fuel, and thus the Turbary Road was constructed for the passage of carts to the Turbary Pasture higher up the fell. Today it serves as a splendid walkers' way, offering a grand prospect of the bulk of Whernside and better still, being perfectly laid out for examination of the caves.

Ingleborough across Twisleton Scars

Strung along the limestone shelf occupied by the peat road, a magnificent series of caves and holes await inspection:—

- Kail Pot - 20 yards distant in a uniform grassy hollow: a deep drop
- Swinsto Hole - an unassuming entrance to an important system
- Turbary Pot - on the path: tiny but distinctive
- Rowten Pot - a visual feast, right on the path and appearing dramatically. The irregular gaping chasm drops no less than 350 feet into the bowels of the earth. Adjacent is a less obvious, more sinister hole. Across the path is the collapsed roof of Rowten Cave: 100 yards up the moor is the entrance, with the dry hole next to it offering a short adventure.
- Jingling Pot - slant up to a tree marking this deep, vertical hole, bedecked with ferns and flowers and swallowing a stream
- Bull Pot - another surprise: an innocuous slit proves to be a deep shaft with neat, fluted sides. Below it is Cow Pot (covered)

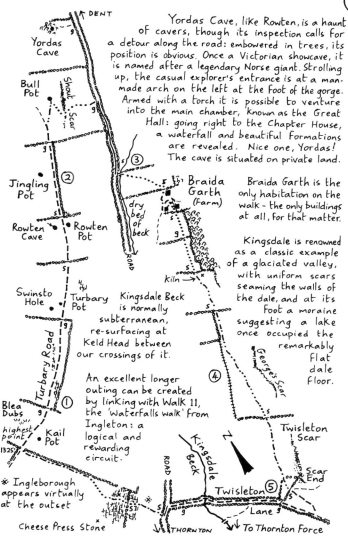

Yordas Cave, like Rowten, is a haunt of cavers, though its inspection calls for a detour along the road: embowered in trees, its position is obvious. Once a Victorian showcase, it is named after a legendary Norse giant. Strolling up, the casual explorer's entrance is at a man-made arch on the left at the foot of the gorge. Armed with a torch it is possible to venture into the main chamber, known as the Great Hall: going right to the Chapter House, a waterfall and beautiful formations are revealed. Nice one, Yordas! The cave is situated on private land.

Braida Garth is the only habitation on the walk – the only buildings at all, for that matter.

Kingsdale is renowned as a classic example of a glaciated valley, with uniform scars seaming the walls of the dale, and at its foot a moraine suggesting a lake once occupied the remarkably flat dale floor.

Kingsdale Beck is normally subterranean, re-surfacing at Keld Head between our crossings of it.

An excellent longer outing can be created by linking with Walk 11, the 'Waterfalls walk' from Ingleton: a logical and rewarding circuit.

✳ Ingleborough appears virtually at the outset

Map labels:
↑ DENT
Yordas Cave
Bull Pot
Shout Scar
Jingling Pot
②
Rowten Cave • Rowten Pot
Swinsto Hole • Turbary Pot
Turbary Road
Blea Dubs
①
highest point
1325'
Kail Pot
Cheese Press Stone
③
Braida Garth (Farm)
dry bed of beck
ROAD
kiln →
George's Scar
④
Twisleton Scar
Scar End
Kingsdale Beck
ROAD
Twisleton ⑤
Lane
THORNTON
To Thornton Force

49

WALK 13

4¾ miles

A simple riverside
stroll of great
charm and
tranquillity

National Park car park
in the village

from Dent

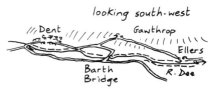

looking south-west

THE WALK

From the car park head along the cobbled street in
the village centre, keeping left at the George and Dragon
to drop down to Church Bridge. Do not use it, but take a
stile on the left to descend to the river. The Dee is hugged
all the way to the walk's turning point, the footbridge at
Ellers. The only breaks are early on, when the Dee nudges us
onto a few yards of road, and approaching Barth Bridge,
where stiles take a more direct course onto the road The
riverbank path resumes on the other side.

Cross the wooden bridge at Ellers and trace the other
bank back until forced up to the road at the monument by a
wooded bank. Turn right to Barth Bridge, and remain on this
bank along an enclosed byway. Shortly after passing a farm
drive (the second one) a stile returns us to the river for the
final yards back to Church Bridge.

Church Bridge

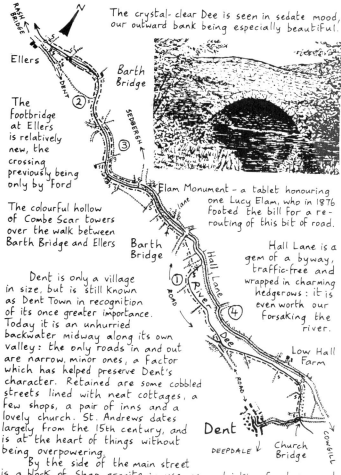

RAISH BRIDGE

N

Ellers

DENT

Barth Bridge

②

SEDBERGH ←

③

The crystal-clear Dee is seen in sedate mood, our outward bank being especially beautiful.

The footbridge at Ellers is relatively new, the crossing previously being only by ford

The colourful hollow of Combe Scar towers over the walk between Barth Bridge and Ellers

Elam Monument – a tablet honouring one Lucy Elam, who in 1876 footed the bill for a re-routing of this bit of road.

Barth Bridge

lane

Hall Lane

①

River Dee

④

ROAD

Hall Lane is a gem of a byway, traffic-free and wrapped in charming hedgerows: it is even worth our forsaking the river.

Dent is only a village in size, but is still known as Dent Town in recognition of its once greater importance. Today it is an unhurried backwater midway along its own valley: the only roads in and out are narrow, minor ones, a factor which has helped preserve Dent's character. Retained are some cobbled streets lined with neat cottages, a few shops, a pair of inns and a lovely church. St. Andrews dates largely from the 15th century, and is at the heart of things without being overpowering.

Low Hall Farm

ROAD

Dent

DEEPDALE ↓

Church Bridge

COWGILL

By the side of the main street is a block of Shap granite in use as a drinking fountain, and carved with the name Adam Sedgwick. Born here in 1785, he spent over 50 years as Professor of Geology at Cambridge: one of the earliest and best in his field, he did much research into the fascinating geology of his own back yard.

WALK 14

5¼ miles

ON WHERNSIDE'S FLANK

From Chapel le Dale

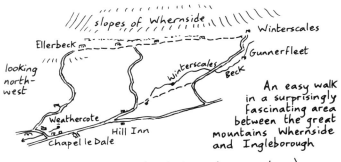

An easy walk in a surprisingly fascinating area between the great mountains Whernside and Ingleborough

Car park at the inn (small charge to non-patrons)

THE WALK

From the Hill Inn head south along the Ingleton road, turning off right within minutes on a road deep into the trees. At the church fork right again up an inviting lane, winding up past Gill Head and across a large open pasture to Ellerbeck. A broad track takes over, along the front of the buildings, across a field and straight on to Bruntscar.

Just beyond the buildings, leave the farm road to go straight ahead to a hand-gate. A thin path crosses the next pasture to Broadrake. Once again pass along the front, and a thin path runs through several fields to join a track to Ivescar. Keep straight on - with most of the buildings on your right - on another farm road until just short of Winterscales, where a branch right crosses a pasture to Gunnerfleet.

Do not cross the beck to it, but remain on the farm road through more fields before it decides to cross the beck. Leave it after a cattle-grid soon after the bridge, a thin path following the wall to a gate on the right. With Gatekirk Cave down to the right, follow the left-hand wall away, and when it departs keep on to the far end, and Haw Gill Wheel.

From the stile follow the wall away, and at a gate an enclosed way (natural line of the beck) leads through to a farm road. Follow it up to the left, past Philpin and out onto the main road just yards below the inn.

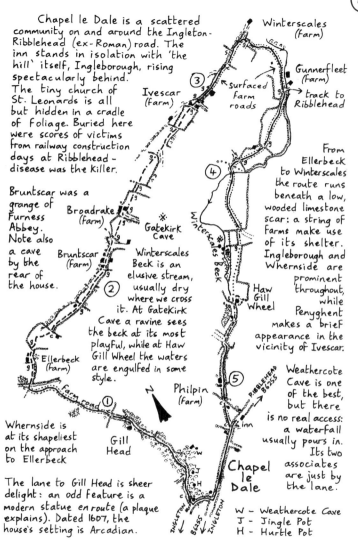

Chapel le Dale is a scattered community on and around the Ingleton-Ribblehead (ex-Roman) road. The inn stands in isolation with 'the hill' itself, Ingleborough, rising spectacularly behind.

The tiny church of St. Leonards is all but hidden in a cradle of foliage. Buried here were scores of victims from railway construction days at Ribblehead - disease was the killer.

Bruntscar was a grange of Furness Abbey. Note also a cave by the rear of the house.

Winterscales Beck is an elusive stream, usually dry where we cross it. At Gatekirk Cave a ravine sees the beck at its most playful, while at Haw Gill Wheel the waters are engulfed in some style.

Whernside is at its shapeliest on the approach to Ellerbeck

The lane to Gill Head is sheer delight: an odd feature is a modern statue en route (a plaque explains). Dated 1607, the house's setting is Arcadian.

From Ellerbeck to Winterscales the route runs beneath a low, wooded limestone scar: a string of farms make use of its shelter. Ingleborough and Whernside are prominent throughout, while Penyghent makes a brief appearance in the vicinity of Ivescar.

Weathercote Cave is one of the best, but there is no real access: a waterfall usually pours in. Its two associates are just by the lane.

Winterscales (Farm)
Gunnerfleet (Farm)
track to Ribblehead
surfaced farm roads
Ivescar (Farm)
Broadrake (Farm)
Gatekirk Cave
Bruntscar (Farm)
Ellerbeck (Farm)
farm road
Gill Head
Philpin (Farm)
Winterscales Beck
Haw Gill Wheel
inn
Chapel le Dale

W - Weathercote Cave
J - Jingle Pot
H - Hurtle Pot

INGLETON
53

The Hill Inn, Chapel le Dale, and Ingleborough

WALK 15

8½ miles

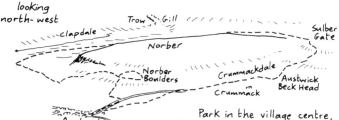

looking
north-west

Trow Gill

Clapdale

Norber

Sulber Gate

Norber Boulders

Crummackdale

Austwick Beck Head

Crummack

Austwick

A limestone classic, with the Norber Boulders a famous exception. Generally easy walking, much being along three unsurfaced green lanes.

Park in the village centre, with care as space is limited.
※ An alternative start-point is Clapham car-park. A glance at the Ordnance map will show how the walk can easily be joined by turning up by the church, under two tunnels to the junction of Thwaite Lane and Long Lane.

THE WALK

From the village centre head east past the inn and left up Townhead Lane. At a crossroads with a rough lane go left along it, but leave almost immediately over a stile on the right to follow a track to a gate. Do not use it, but accompany the wall up to a stile in the corner. Climb the slope behind to a guidepost, to which we shall soon return. For now though, continue up to where a path squeezes between limestone outcrops then fades on the Norber Boulders plateau.

After exploring the attractions return to the post and turn right on a sketchy path above a wall and below Robin Proctor's Scar. Beyond a stile the wall turns sharp left, while our path heads half-left across a large pasture to a stile back onto Thwaite Lane. Turn right along this walled track to a T-junction, then here turn right again along the similarly Roman-like Long Lane. Living up to its name, remain on it to its eventual demise into a green pasture.

Now turn up to the right on a track rising to a stile. Beyond it the track continues more clearly as it wends its way past Long Scar. Avoiding any lesser deviations, a wall-junction at Sulber Gate is eventually reached. Don't use the gate or even the adjacent stile, but opt for the smaller gate in the right-hand wall. A path descends to Thieves Moss: passing between moss and limestone it forks, the cairned right-hand path passing a variety of outcrops and running near the edge of a natural amphitheatre before dropping to Beggar's Stile.

Over the stile a path descends, soon becoming vague but maintaining its direction. An equally sketchy path diverts left to visit Austwick Beck Head, its location being fairly obvious. Back on the original path a stile is soon reached, with Crummack Farm just beyond. Here a gate in the wall in front avoids the farm, and its access road is joined to lead unerringly back to Austwick.

Long Lane runs parallel with Clapdale down to the left, and provides good views of Ingleborough Cave, Trow Gill, and Ingleborough's summit plateau.

Thwaite Scars

Long Lane

③

to/from Clapham (see note on page 55)

Thwaite Lane

②

* A varied finish can be had by leaving Crummack Lane after it becomes surfaced, at a stile on the left. Drop to a stile by a barn then rise to join a rough lane. Cross straight over, head away with the wall to a stile onto a drive, then through small gates between houses onto Townhead Lane.

Unfortunately there is no public right-of-way onto the very top of Norber (1320'), though one does run to a stile to give access to it!

Former tarn   Robin Proctor's Scar   Norber Boulders

Crummack Lane

①

⑧

As soon as Thwaite Lane is left, the Norber boulder-field comes into view, with the prominent Robin Proctor's Scar just to the left

Austwick

The map includes a short-cut from Crummack Lane to the boulders, tailor-made for those using the Clapham start.

CLAPHAM ←
SETTLE ←
→ HELWITH BRIDGE

56

Austwick is a hugely attractive village, happily set well back from the main A65 road. A small green, a particularly cosy inn, a centuries-old hall and countless tidy cottages combine to create a picture of great charm.

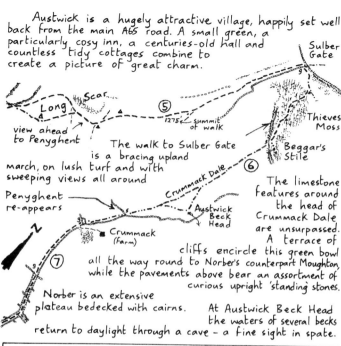

Long Scar

view ahead to Penyghent

Sulber Gate

summit of walk

Thieves Moss

Beggar's Stile

The walk to Sulber Gate is a bracing upland march, on lush turf and with sweeping views all around

Crummack Dale

Penyghent re-appears

Austwick Beck Head

The limestone features around the head of Crummack Dale are unsurpassed. A terrace of cliffs encircle this green bowl all the way round to Norber's counterpart Moughton, while the pavements above bear an assortment of curious upright 'standing stones.

Crummack (Farm)

Norber is an extensive plateau bedecked with cairns. At Austwick Beck Head the waters of several becks return to daylight through a cave – a fine sight in spate.

The Norber Boulders are geological freaks, famous specimens of something that the Ice Age brought in. A retreating glacier carried rocks from further up Crummack Dale and deposited them in their present position. What is so special is that they are dark Silurian rocks, now atop white limestone pedestals that have worn away more rapidly.

They are termed 'erratic', and are a bit special.

A Norber erratic

WALK 16

9½ miles

From Horton-in-Ribblesdale

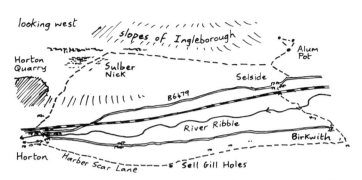

looking west • slopes of Ingleborough • Alum Pot • Horton Quarry • Sulber Nick • Selside • B6479 • River Ribble • Birkwith • Horton • Harber Scar Lane • Sell Gill Holes

An extended limestone ramble on both sides of the Ribble

National Park car park in the village centre

THE WALK

Leave the village by the rough Harber Scar Lane up the side of the Crown Hotel. It rises steadily across the lower flanks of Penyghent, eventually running part-unenclosed to Sell Gill Holes. Through the gate behind, the broad track of the Pennine Way is left by crossing to a stile just along to the left. Go past the barn and turn at once along to the right, to commence a long, level walk on a broad shelf.

A sketchy trail is evident for much of the way, which after a long pasture becomes briefly enclosed to emerge below an old limekiln. On again, a slight rise to a stile leads along to a surprisingly deep-cut gill. Up the other side, at last desert the terrace by rising steadily right, latching onto another grassy shelf below a scar to meet a broad track above a wooded ravine. Go left to a junction just below Old Ing, and turn down the stony road to High Birkwith Farm.

Here the terminus of the road from Horton is joined, but only for 30 yards before taking a stile on the right. Crossing to a strip plantation, the way emerges to slant down to the farm at Low Birkwith, in view below. Meeting Coppy Gill at the first enclosure, keep with the beck to the yard at the front of the house. Cross straight over to a gate, and keeping the barns on the left, return to shadow the beck downstream again. A simple bridge eventually crosses it to gain access to a wooden footbridge across the Ribble itself. Swinging around the base of the hill behind, the head of a walled lane is reached. This is the well-named – in its early stages, at least – Drain Mires Lane, and it strikes unerringly up into Selside.

After passing under the railway, the white-walled Selside Farm on the right is the place to pay your nominal fee if wishing to explore the environs of Alum Pot, just a little further ahead (Alum Pot and its neighbours are situated wholly on private land). Whether doing so or not, turn right along the main road, out of the hamlet and then left at a rough lane. At its far end a contrasting green lane strikes off, and this is the continuation of the route. In front is a stile, however, and if you've paid your pennies, set off to sample the wonders of cave country – see overleaf.

Back at the stile, the woefully short-lived green lane is superceded by a faint track, swinging left at a wall-corner towards Gill Garth Farm. Though the track improves, leave it by going straight ahead to a ladder-stile, and on through two more to the foot of an extensive pasture. A broad green way sets forth up its gentle slope: the ultimate target is the far top corner, reached by linking several such ways. From the top stile a level track runs on to Sulber's crossroads.

Taking the advice of the firmly embedded guidepost, head for Horton on the final stage of the walk. A well-worn path runs through the distinct trough of Sulber Nick, the wayward staggering of Three Peak-sloggers being evident in the state of the path after a wet spell.

All in good time the path meets its first stile, to begin the drop through limestone scars towards Horton, part of which is now visible ahead. Slanting half-right the path leaves the outcrops behind for the final few fields, crossing the drive to Beecroft Hall and surmounting one final brow before descending over the railway line and back into the village.

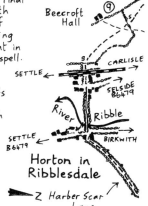

For a note on Horton see Walk 1

Sulber is a notable crossroads of walkers' ways, and the highest point of this walk. Here the path ascending Ingleborough from Horton crosses the Austwick-Selside bridleway, facilitating two less frequented starts to the climb. The guidepost's distance to Horton is a trifle optimistic.

Sulber
1214'

A shooting-box (not seen) above Sulber indicates that not many decades ago much of the higher ground was grouse moor

⑦

Sulber Nick

A pronounced trench alongside limestone scars

Borrins (Farm)

⑧

Alum Pot Beck enters the hole in spectacular fashion after a wet spell

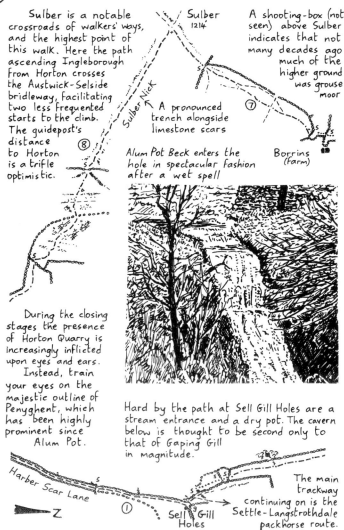

During the closing stages the presence of Horton Quarry is increasingly inflicted upon eyes and ears. Instead, train your eyes on the majestic outline of Penyghent, which has been highly prominent since Alum Pot.

Hard by the path at Sell Gill Holes are a stream entrance and a dry pot. The cavern below is thought to be second only to that of Gaping Gill in magnitude.

Harber Scar Lane

⟵ Z

①

Sell Gill Holes

The main trackway continuing on is the Settle-Langstrothdale packhorse route.

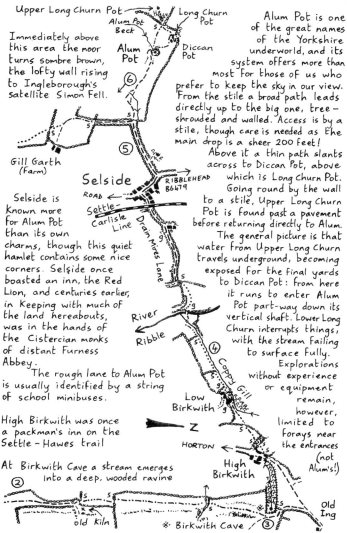

Upper Long Churn Pot → → Long Churn Pot

Alum Pot Beck

Alum Pot

Diccan Pot

Immediately above this area the moor turns sombre brown, the lofty wall rising to Ingleborough's satellite Simon Fell.

Alum Pot is one of the great names of the Yorkshire underworld, and its system offers more than most for those of us who prefer to keep the sky in our view. From the stile a broad path leads directly up to the big one, tree-shrouded and walled. Access is by a stile, though care is needed as the main drop is a sheer 200 feet!

Above it a thin path slants across to Diccan Pot, above which is Long Churn Pot. Going round by the wall to a stile, Upper Long Churn Pot is found past a pavement before returning directly to Alum. The general picture is that water from Upper Long Churn travels underground, becoming exposed for the final yards to Diccan Pot : from here it runs to enter Alum Pot part-way down its vertical shaft. Lower Long Churn interrupts things, with the stream failing to surface fully.

Explorations without experience or equipment remain, however, limited to forays near the entrances (not Alum's!)

Gill Garth (Farm)

Selside

RIBBLEHEAD B6479

ROAD ←

Settle-Carlisle Line

Drain Mires Lane

Selside is known more for Alum Pot than its own charms, though this quiet hamlet contains some nice corners. Selside once boasted an inn, the Red Lion, and centuries earlier, in keeping with much of the land hereabouts, was in the hands of the Cistercian monks of distant Furness Abbey.

The rough lane to Alum Pot is usually identified by a string of school minibuses.

High Birkwith was once a packman's inn on the Settle - Hawes trail

River Ribble

Coppy Gill

Low Birkwith

HORTON ←

High Birkwith

Old Ing

At Birkwith Cave a stream emerges into a deep, wooded ravine

② old Kiln

✱ Birkwith Cave ③

LOG OF THE WALKS

These two pages provide an opportunity to maintain a permanent record of the walks completed

WALK	DATE	TIME Start	Finish	WEATHER	COMMENTS
1					
2					
3					
4					
5					
6					
7					
8					

WALK	DATE	TIME Start	TIME Finish	WEATHER	COMMENTS	
9						
10						
11						
12						
13						
14						
15						
16						

KEY TO THE MAP SYMBOLS

direction of north

scale
2½ inches = 1 mile (approx)

Route — clear — sketchy — no visible path

Route on public road — unenclosed — wall — fence/hedge

River/beck — bridge

Marsh

Peat grough

Crags

Limestone clints

Loose rocks/ scree

Cairns
summit   other

Trees

Buildings

Church

Abbreviations
c = cattle grid
s = stile
g = gate

Miles from start
③

THE COUNTRY CODE

Respect the life and work of the countryside
Protect wildlife, plants and trees
Keep to public paths across farmland
Safeguard water supplies
Go carefully on country roads
Keep dogs under control
Guard against all risks of fire
Fasten all gates
Leave no litter - take it with you
Make no unnecessary noise
Leave livestock, crops and machinery alone
Use gates and stiles to cross fences, hedges
and walls